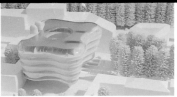 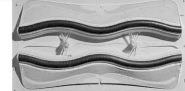 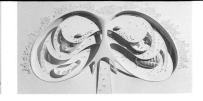 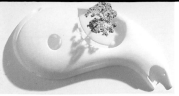 

To say it is beyond the capabilities of the conventional construction industry to build such an object is to state the obvious. It is beyond conventional construction in the same way as advanced technology is beyond "High-Tech". This capsule building is an industrial product, a modular, computer dimensioned and cut aluminium hull, fabricated in sections in a Cornish shipyard, its segments trucked to London and welded together on site. Like cars, boats and aeroplanes it has few right angles and many compound curves. From its inclined optical glazing to its glistening white skin, every aspect of this revolutionary building has been honed by 20 years of single minded monocoque design development, so that its originals can be traced back to Jan Kaplicky's earliest capsule projects of the 1970s. The completion of the NatWest Media Centre will represent a breakthrough in architectural design comparable to the advent of the Willis Faber Dumas building or the Farnsworth House.

Every machine can lose its identity in function, and so it is with the Future Systems designs that have yet to be built. Project 224 The Ark, the Millennium Fund-financed central exhibition space for the Doncaster Earth Centre, embodies magnificent concentrations of organic technology. Its twin elliptical diagrid roofs, contained by tubular steel ring beams, double as complex light machines, made up of thousands of internal and external super plastic aluminium scoops graduating in colour chameleon-like from red to orange to yellow. Spread across a 120 metre wide

exhibition space, the purpose of these insect-eye like assemblies is to deny south light to the spacious 10,000 m^2 interior; reflect north light into it, and serve as mountings for the innumerable photovoltaic cells that will generate its power.

From the Lord's Media Centre and the Ark, via projects in London and Berlin for "Zero Emission Developments" for the European Commission, via the brilliantly successful Docklands Bridge and the project for a habitable Thames bridge, via Hallfield School and Bedford School – two projects that evolved new classrooms and a new teaching environment – Future Systems stands today on the brink of a success that is all the more deserved for being so long delayed. Despite a glorious history of publications and competition success over the years, Future Systems only really broke through the paper ceiling with Project 180, the Islington house they designed for Debra Hauer and Jeremy King. It is part of the mythology of advanced technology architecture that this house was sold at a considerable profit.

Since the Hauer-King house another house commission has come their way, a dwelling that is now nearing completion on a cliff top in the Pembrokeshire Coast National Park. Semi-elliptical in plan, dug-in to its slope, its stressed skin roof covered with earth, grass and gorse, it has a 24 metre glass wall facing out to sea. The surrounding landscape is untouched and the house itself is barely visible. Project 222, as with all of Future System's work, is a commentary on the proper relationship of technology and nature.

From left to right:
Project Zed, Toulouse, 1995;
Project Zed, Berlin, 1995;
The Ark at the Earth Centre, 1995;
Cambridge House, 1997;
Bedford School, 1998

1993
**Gallery for the
21st Century**

A collaboration between
Future Systems and Ove Arup
& Partners to conceptualise
in a built form the idea of a
gallery for the 21st century
on the site of the old

Bankside Power Station.
The driving force of the
scheme is the control
of daylight to illuminate
the art. A vast volume of
space under a single

elegant roof provides an
enhanced setting for art
works. External shells
ensure only north light is let
into the space with reverse
fabric shells internally

reflecting this light deep
into the floor plates.

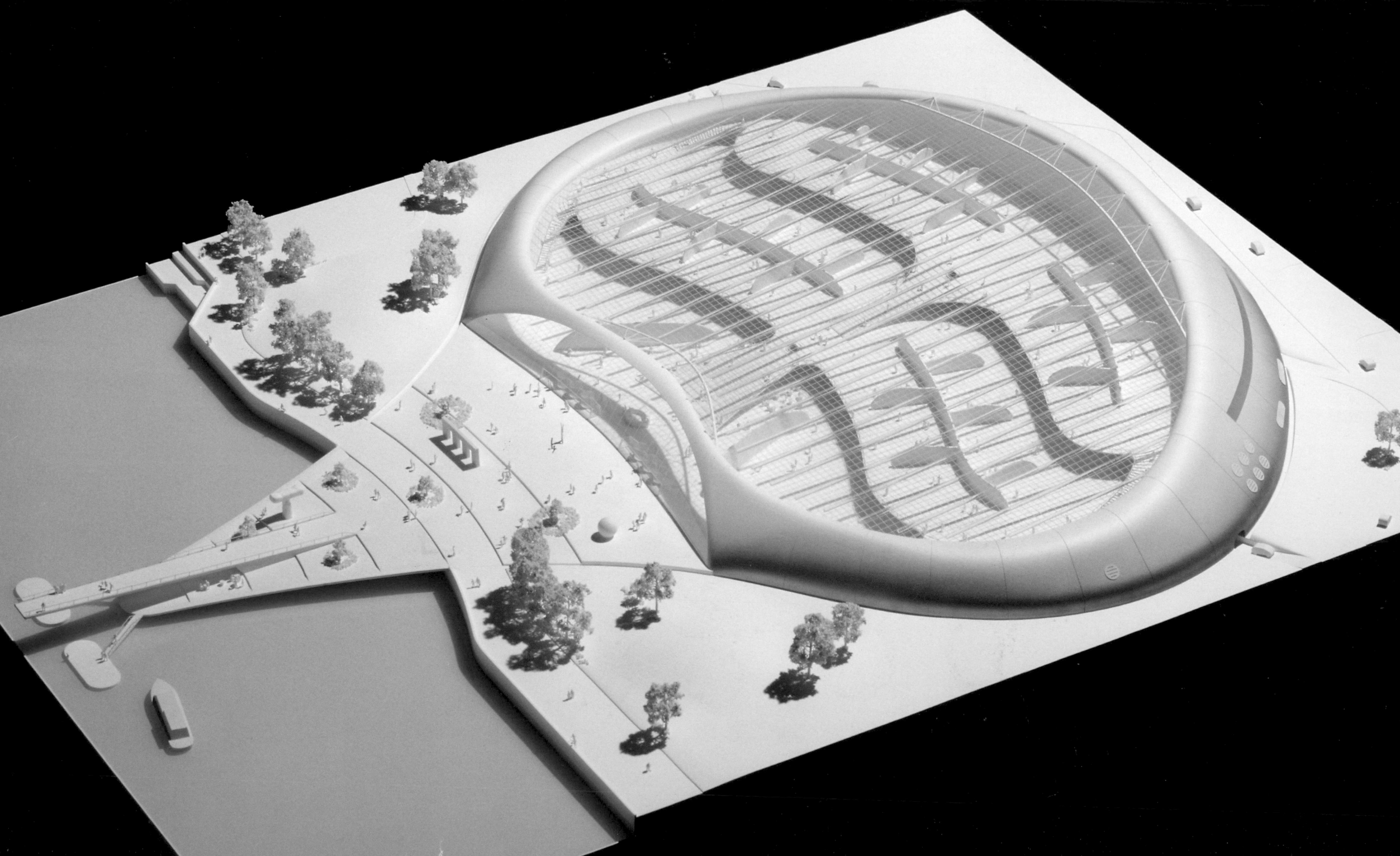

Superbus

Superbus is a response to many years of uncomfortable and noisy journeys on London buses. This low slung bus is an aluminium semi-monocoque structure which allows a completely uninterrupted floor area with a capacity of 90 passengers. The sleek elegance of the body work is achieved by exploiting the innovative construction technique of the monocoque. Electric motors are positioned on the wheels for efficiency and the batteries are rechargeable at terminus points. The entire bus lowers at bus stops allowing the elderly and disabled easy access.

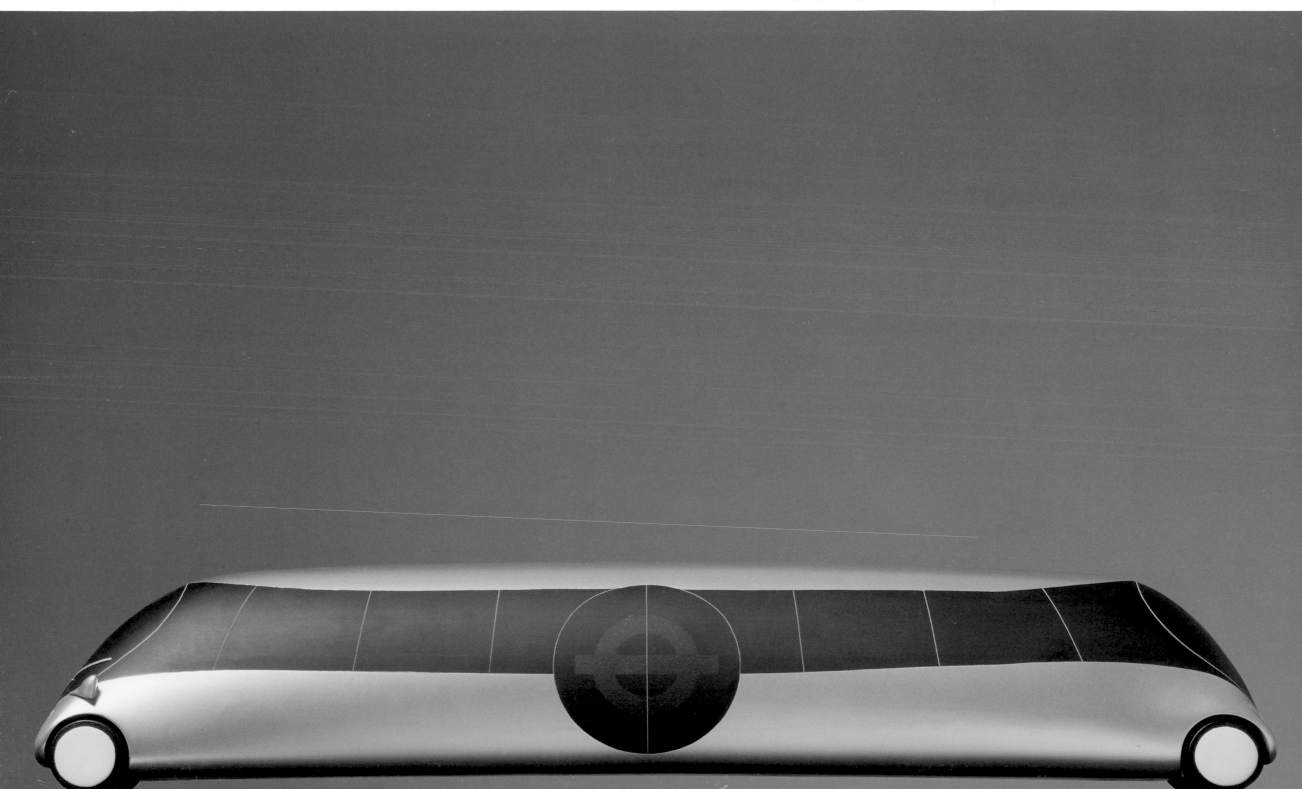

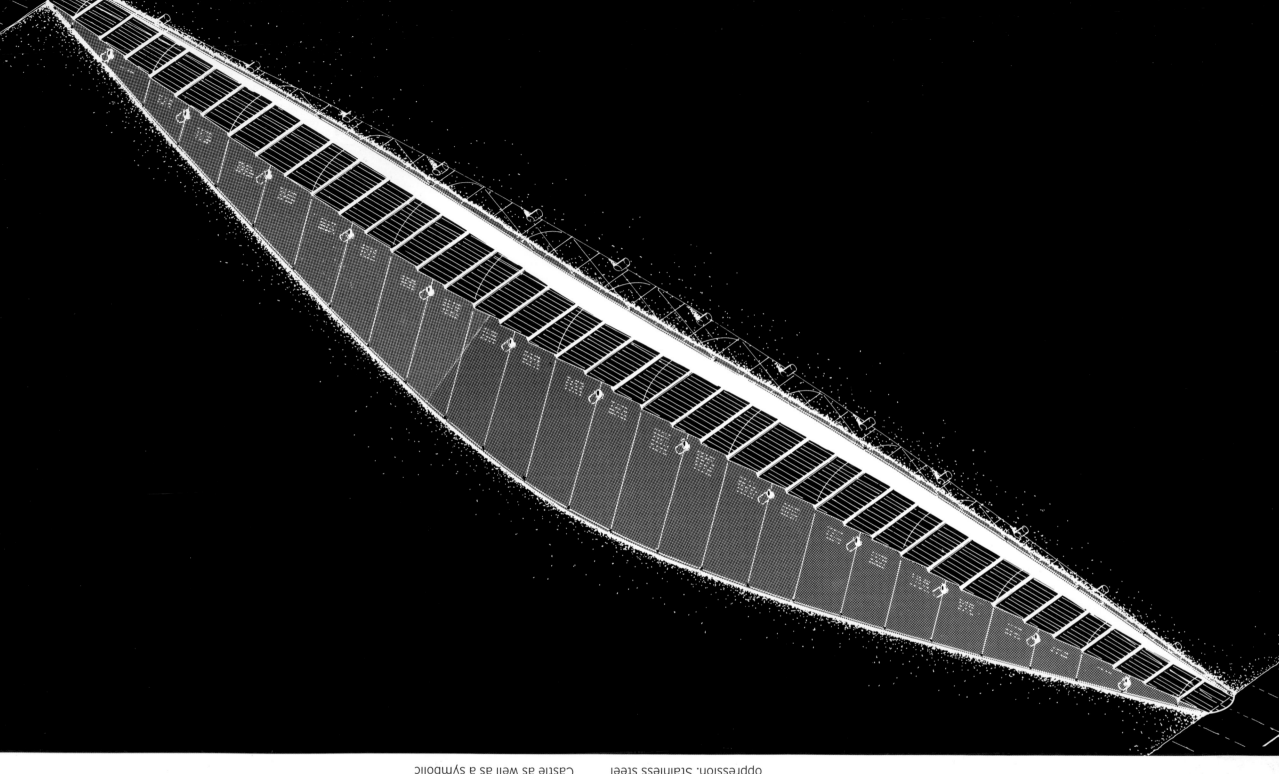

1993 **Memorial Prague**

A memorial to the victims of the communist dictatorship in Czechoslovakia between 1948-1989, 42 steps mark 42 years of physical oppression. Stainless steel steps span between a cut in the slopes of Letenska Plateau creating a pedestrian route between the Old Town and Prague Castle as well as a symbolic marker for the years of political oppression.

Floating Bridge

The bridge links two areas of very different scale; on the one side a vast commercial development and on the other the more delicate proportions of 19th century warehouses. By creating a low floating structure, emphasis is placed on the horizontal stretch of water rather than the vertical dominance of Canary Wharf.

The slender delicate form of the bridge is evocative of a brightly coloured insect touching the water as lightly as a waterskater. Colour is central to the concept - like a laser beam of light, the bridge skims the dock with a piercing lime green line, the sense of perspective exaggerated by the tapering plan of the deck.

There exists at Lord's
Cricket Ground a tradition
of patronage of innovative
structures – the objective
of this design has been to
respect and savour the

essential nature of Lord's
while bringing to it a building
that will herald the coming
millennium and provide
the most elegant and state-
of-the-art media centre in

the world. An entirely
aluminium semi-monocoque
structure, fabricated
and fitted out by boat
builders, this building is
a synthesis of the work

and ideas of Future Systems
over many years.

House in Wales

The site is in a very sensitive area within the Pembrokeshire National Park – it's dramatic location and the beauty of the surroundings have been the driving force of the design. The building appears to be a natural part of the topography with the soft, organic form melting into the rugged grass landscape. Both the roof and the sides of the house are turfed with local vegetation. An elliptical eye of clear glass overlooks the Atlantic maximising the stunning views of the Welsh coastline.

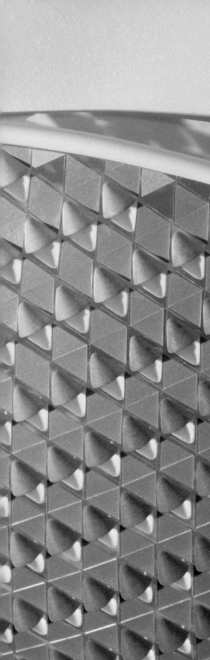

A building that is soft and organic to enclose the energy-efficient, non-polluting technologies of the 21st century, The Ark, the centrepiece building at

the Earth Centre, is a vast 10,000 m² exhibition hall housing exhibits and rides on the theme of a sustainable future – translating ideas, research and world events

into a language that will reach the hearts and minds of many. The highly coloured roof made up of hundreds of shell-like forms, is a living, breathing skin of energy

generating photovoltaic panels allowing almost the entire building to be naturally lit.

This bridge, spanning between Embankment Gardens and the South Bank, is a place to go – a place to meet – a place from which to see London – a place to be seen. The fluid and organic form echoes the natural forces of the river tides. People are able to walk inside and on top of the bridge, animating the route across the water. The introduction of colour to the skin creates a dynamic image and accentuates the slender, elegant curves of the form.

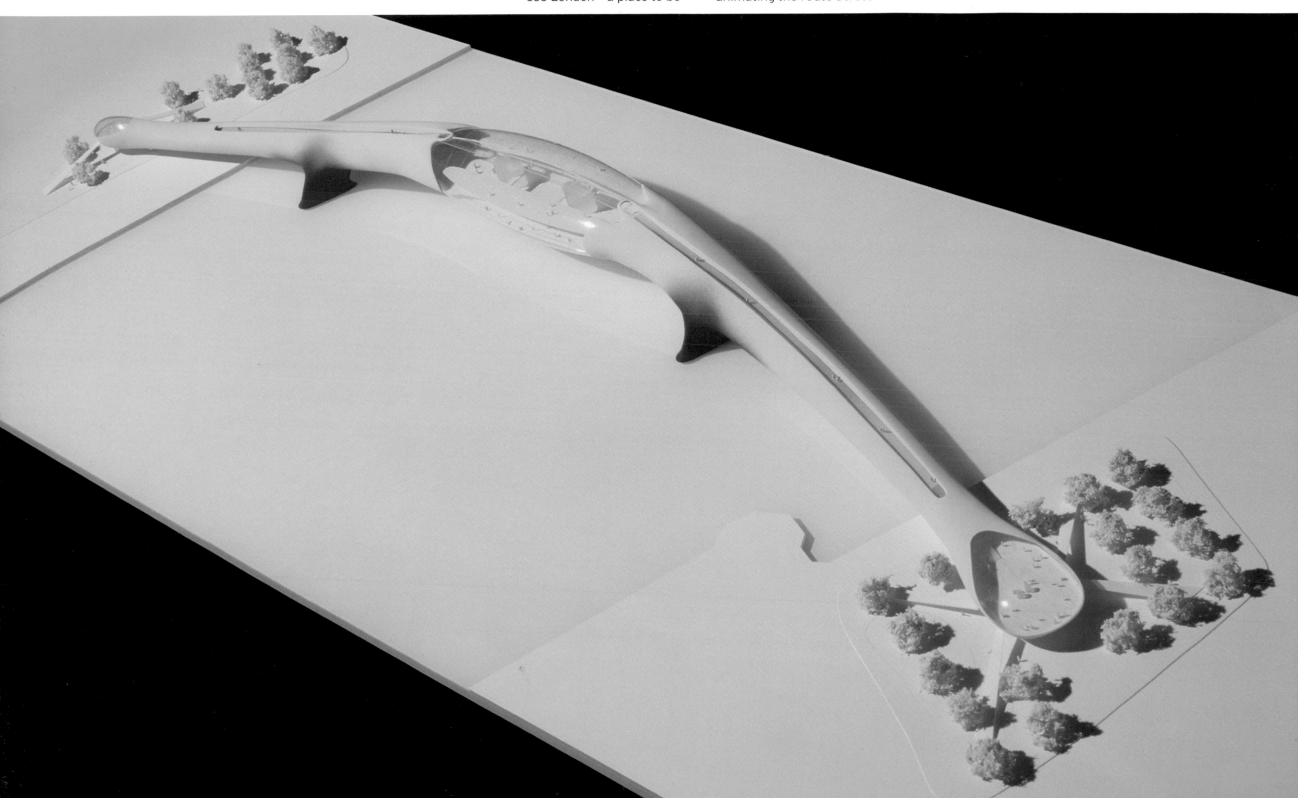

In 1951 Sir Denys Lasdun used the motif of an unfurling plant to describe the concept of his design for Hallfield School. His organic analogy has also been the guiding force in this design, adding leaves to the plant linked by a transparent stem - little pavilions for little people. But this scheme is more than just a solution to the lack of space at Hallfield. It is an opportunity to propose a high quality, prefabricated system of circular, top lit classroom units that could be used for schools and nurseries up and down the country.

Wild at Heart

Flowers are not about straight lines - they are organic structures whose forms change as they grow. The design of the shop reflects the fluidity of these forms. Flowers are displayed in a couture environment. Gently curved cascading terraces increase the sense of perspective and the whiteness of the interior provides a dramatic backdrop in stark contrast to the vivid colours of the flowers themselves. A splash of yellow defines the area of soft seating. Projected in front of the historic facade is a glass shield forming the new shop front, making a legible distinction between old and new.

Future Systems

Future Systems is an
architectural and design
practice founded by
**Jan Kaplicky in 1979.
Amanda Levete joined as
a partner in 1989 and
David Miller and
Angus Pond were made
associates in 1997**

**Future Systems
past and present**
Lindy Atkin
Jonathan Clark
Kate Francis
Katy Ghahremani
David Grinaway
David Hayhurst
Matthew Heywood
Mark Jackson
Jan Kaplicky
Billie Lee
Amanda Levete
David Miller
Simon Mitchell
Mark Newton
David Nixon
Angus Pond
Rachel Stevenson
Anthony St Leger

Selected Solo Exhibitions
'For Inspiration Only', Architecture
Foundation, London 1996

'Floating Bridge, West India Quay',
Architectural Association,
London 1996

'Gallery for the 21st Century',
Concord Gallery, London &
Gallery O, Stockholm 1995

'Future Systems: Recent Work',
Storefront, New York 1992

'Future Systems: Architecture',
RIBA, London 1991

'Future Systems Drawings',
River Cafe, London 1998

'Future Systems', Rice University,
Houston 1998

'Future Systems',
Architectural Association,
London 1987

'Future Systems', Graham
Foundation, Chicago 1987

'Future Systems', RIBA 1982

Selected Group Exhibitions
'New Urban Environments',
Tokyo 1998

'Cities of the Future',
Hong Kong 1997

'Living Bridges', Royal Academy,
London 1996

'Royal Academy Summer Show'
1990, 1993, 1995, 1996

'Contemporary British
Architecture', Los Angeles,
New York, Chicago 1995

'Bibliothèque de France',
IFA, Paris 1989

'Temps Sauvage et Incertain',
IFA, Paris 1989

'Metropolis', ICA, London 1988

'Nouvelles Tendances',
Centre Pompidou, Paris 1987

'Vision der Moderne',
Deutsches Architekturmuseum,
Frankfurt 1983

Selected TV
BBC2 Building Sites:
'Glass House' 1995

Channel 4 Without Walls:
'House of Glass' 1994

BBC2 Late Show:
'Future Systems Architecture' 1991

Selected Awards
British Construction Industry
Award, Small Project Award,
Floating Bridge, 1997

Civic Trust Award,
Floating Bridge, 1997

Financial Times Award,
Highly Commended,
Floating Bridge, 1997

Civic Trust Award,
Hauer-King House, 1996

Aluminium Imagination
Award, 1st prize,
Hauer-King House, 1995

AJ/Bovis Royal Academy
Award, 1st prize,
Stonehenge Visitor Centre, 1993

British Construction Industry
Award, Highly Commended,
MOMI Tent, 1992

Publications
'Hauer-King House',
Architecture in Detail by
Martin Pawley, Phaidon 1997

'For Inspiration Only',
Academy Editions 1996

'Future Systems - Story of
Tomorrow' by Martin Pawley,
Phaidon 1993

'Future Systems',
Architectural Association 1987

Models
Unit 22
A Models
Arup Modelshop

Photography
Richard Davies
Geoff Beekman
Peter Mackinven